I0448782

Congressional
Research Service
Informing the legislative debate since 1914 _____

International Corporate Tax Rate Comparisons and Policy Implications

Jane G. Gravelle

Senior Specialist in Economic Policy

January 6, 2014

Congressional Research Service

7-5700

www.crs.gov

R41743

Summary

Advocates of cutting corporate tax rates frequently make their argument based on the higher statutory rate in the United States as compared with the rest of the world; they argue that cutting corporate taxes would induce large investment flows into the United States, which would create jobs or expand the taxable income base enough to raise revenue. President Barack Obama has supported a rate cut if the revenue loss can be offset with corporate base broadening. Others have urged on one hand, a revenue raising reform, and, on the other, setting deficit concerns aside.

Is the U.S. tax rate higher than the rest of the world, and what does that difference imply for tax policy? The answer depends, in part, on which tax rates are being compared. Although the U.S. statutory tax rate is higher, the average effective rate is about the same, and the marginal rate on new investment is only slightly higher. The statutory rate differential is relevant for international profit shifting; effective rates are more relevant for firms' investment levels. The 13.7 percentage point differential in statutory rates (a 39.2% rate for the United States compared with 25.5% in other countries), narrows to about 9 percentage points when tax rates in the rest of the world are weighted to reflect the size of countries' economies. (The OECD rates fell by slightly over one-half of a percentage point between 2010 and 2012.)

Regardless of tax differentials, could a U.S. rate cut lead to significant economic gains and revenue feedbacks? Because of the factors that constrain capital flows, estimates for a rate cut from 35% to 25% suggest a modest positive effect on wages and output: an eventual one-time increase of less than two-tenths of 1% of output. Most of this output gain is not an increase in national income because returns to capital imported from abroad belong to foreigners and the returns to U.S. investment abroad that comes back to the United States are already owned by U.S. firms.

The revenue cost of such a rate cut is estimated at between $1.2 trillion and $1.5 trillion over the next 10 years. Revenue feedback effects from increased investment inflows are estimated to reduce those revenue costs by 5%-6%. Reductions in profit shifting could have larger effects, but even if profit shifting disappeared entirely, it would not likely offset revenue losses. It seems unlikely that a rate cut to 25% would significantly reduce profit shifting given these transactions are relatively costless and largely constrained by laws, enforcement, and court decisions.

Both output gains and revenue offsets would be reduced if other countries responded to a U.S. rate cut by reducing their own taxes. Evidence suggests that the U.S. rate cut in the Tax Reform Act of 1986 triggered rate cuts in other countries.

It is difficult, although not impossible, to design a reform to lower the corporate tax rate by 10 percentage points that is revenue neutral in the long run. Standard tax expenditures do not appear adequate for this purpose. Eliminating one of the largest provisions, accelerated depreciation, gains much more revenue in the short run than in the long run, and a long-run revenue-neutral change would increase the cost of capital. Other revisions, such as restricting foreign tax credits and interest deductibility or increasing shareholder level taxes, may be required.

This report focuses on the global issues relating to tax rate differentials between the United States and other countries. It provides tax rate comparisons; discusses policy implications, including the effect of a corporate rate cut on revenue, output, and national welfare; and discusses the outlook for and consequences of a revenue neutral corporate tax reform.

Contents

Figures

Tables

Appendixes

Contacts

A dvocates of cutting corporate tax rates frequently make their argument based on the higher statutory rate observed in the United States as compared with the rest of the world.[1] Sometimes the higher rate alone is used as an argument, and in other cases the arguments include claims that cutting corporate taxes would induce large investment flows into the United States, which would create jobs or expand the base enough to raise revenue.

President Barack Obama has supported a rate cut if the revenue loss can be offset with corporate base broadening, while the Citizens for Tax Justice has urged a revenue raising reform and business leaders have urged setting deficit concerns aside.[2] House Majority Leader Eric Cantor has also proposed a 25% corporate rate in the context of tax reform and Ways and Means Chairman Dave Camp has proposed a 25% combined with a move to a territorial tax system.[3]

Many issues arise regarding the corporate tax outside of the global perspective addressed in other reports.[4] This report focuses on the global issue relating to tax rate differentials between the United States and other countries. The first section provides tax rate comparisons. The second section discusses policy implications, including the effect of a corporate rate cut on revenue, output, and national welfare; the possibility that a rate cut may induce reactions from other countries; and the outlook for and consequences of a revenue-neutral corporate tax reform.

Effective Tax Rate Comparisons

Several important features affect the interpretation of the comparative tax rates: the type of rate, what taxes are included, and the use of weighted measures to adjust for size differences. A number of tax rate comparisons follow the discussion of these features.

---

[1] These advocates include several economists. For example, see Kevin Hassett, "Let's Cut Corporate Taxes to Create More Jobs," *Bloomberg*, January 9, 2006, http://www.bloomberg.com/apps/news?pid=newsarchive&cid=hassett&sid=aZDVcYUY1j2c and "Laffer Curve Pays Billions If Obama Just Asks," *Bloomberg Business Week*, February, 13, 2011, http://www.businessweek.com/news/2011-02-13/laffer-curve-pays-billions-if-obama-just-asks-kevin-hassett html; Robert Carroll, "Comparing International Corporate Tax Rates: U.S. Corporate Tax Rate Increasingly Out of Line by Various Measures," Tax Foundation, *Fiscal Facts*, no. 143, August 28, 2008, http://www.taxfoundation.org/publications/show/23561 html; Duanjie Chen and Jack Mintz, "New Estimates of Effective Corporate Tax Rates on Business Investment," *CATO Institute Tax and Budget Bulletin*, no. 64, February 24, 2011, http://www.cato.org/pubs/tbb/tbb_64.pdf, and Curtis Dubay, "Corporate Tax Reform Should Focus on Rate Reduction ,"The Heritage Foundation, February 11, 2011, http://www heritage.org/Research/Reports/2011/02/Corporate-Tax-Reform-Should-Focus-on-Rate-Reduction.

[2] See "Obama Backs Corporate Tax Cut If Won't Raise Deficit," *Bloomberg*, January 25, 2011, http://www.bloomberg.com/news/2011-01-26/obama-backs-cut-in-u-s-corporate-tax-rate-only-if-it-won-t-affect-deficit html.

[3] See "Leader Cantor Unveils Pro-Growth Economic Plan at Stanford University," press release, March 21, 2011, http://majorityleader house.gov/newsroom/2011/03/embargoed-leader-cantor-unveils-pro-growth-economic-plan-at-stanford-university.html. See CRS Report R42624, *Moving to a Territorial Income Tax: Options and Challenges*, by Jane G. Gravelle, for a discussion of the Camp proposal.

[4] See CRS Report RL34229, *Corporate Tax Reform: Issues for Congress*, by Jane G. Gravelle, for a more general discussion of corporate tax issues. In general, the corporate tax contributes revenue and progressivity to the tax system as well as protecting the individual income tax base by preventing or limiting the use of the corporation as a tax shelter. It imposes costs in distortions in the allocation of capital between the corporate and noncorporate sector, the use of debt versus equity finance, and savings behavior. Although the tax creates a savings distortion, it probably has a limited effect on the size of the domestic capital stock, because of income and substitution effects.

Types of Tax Rates

Three basic types of tax rates are reported: the statutory rate, the effective rate, and the marginal effective rate. The statutory rate is the rate in the tax statute; in the case of the United States, it is the top marginal corporate tax rate of 35%. The effective rate is determined by the ratio of taxes paid divided by profits. The effective rate captures the tax benefits that reduce the taxable income base relative to financial profits. The marginal tax rate is calculated from a projected investment project: it estimates the share of the pre-tax return that is paid in taxes.

Each type of tax rate has its advantages and disadvantages, and is useful for considering certain types of behavior. For example, the statutory rate would potentially affect firms' attempts to shift profits by altering the source of borrowing or transferring assets or products at prices that are not arm's length.[5] Even the statutory rate, however, needs some adjustments for this purpose. For example, most multinational firms in the United States are eligible for the production activities deduction, which reduces the U.S. statutory tax rate by 9%, from 35% to 31.85%.

The effective tax rate is taxes paid divided by profits. The effective tax rate captures some of the tax benefits and subsidies, reducing the tax paid per dollar of profit. This measure can make a country with a high statutory rate but narrow base more comparable to a country with a low tax rate and broad base. It is probably more suited to assessing the true relative burdens on investment than the statutory tax rate. However, these types of tax rates may not capture timing effects (such as accelerated depreciation) very well and generally depend on accounting measures of profit that may vary across countries.

The marginal effective tax rate is, in theory, the appropriate measure for determining the effects of tax rate differentials on investment. However, in some cases marginal tax rates do not include all of the components of investment; frequently, they are restricted to investment in fixed assets or fixed assets and inventory. This report estimates an overall marginal effective tax rate that includes inventories and intangibles as well as buildings and equipment. Marginal tax rates also depend on estimates of economic depreciation, expected inflation, and rates of return.

Also briefly discussed is a measure referred to as the effective average tax rate. The implications of this tax rate, which combines statutory and marginal effective rates, are not clear.

Types of Taxes Included

Most tax measures reflect the effect of both national and sub-national corporate income taxes. Of the 31 Organisation for Economic Co-operation and Development (OECD) countries, 8 countries (Canada, Germany, Japan, South Korea, Luxembourg, Portugal, Switzerland, and the United States) have sub-national corporate taxes. In some cases, these sub-national taxes are more significant than those in the United States. In the case of the United States, these corporate income taxes imposed by the state increase the statutory rate (without the production activities deduction) to 39.2%. With the production activities deduction, the combined rate is 36.3%.[6]

---

[5] An arm's length price is the price that would occur for sales or asset transfers between unrelated firms.

[6] The combined rate without the production activities deduction is 0.392 which implies a state tax rate of 0.0646 (solving the equation $0.35 + x(1-0.35) = 0.392$). With the production activities deduction the U.S. rate is 0.3185 and the combined rate is $.3185 + .0646*(1-.3185) = 0.363$, or 36.3%.

Countries can also have other taxes that impose a burden on capital. In the United States, these taxes are imposed by the states and localities, and they include property taxes, franchise taxes, and retail sales taxes that apply to capital goods. These taxes are much more difficult to measure and are generally not included in comparative tax rate measures, although one study (discussed below) includes franchise, and transfer and sales taxes, but not property or wealth taxes.

Simple (Unweighted) versus Weighted Averages of Tax Rates

Another issue that affects the comparisons between U.S. and worldwide tax rates is whether tax rates are simple (unweighted) averages or whether they are weighted in some fashion to indicate their relative importance. If tax rates are not weighted, then a small economy, such as Iceland, can have the same effect on the average of international rates as a large economy, such as Germany or Japan. In general, smaller countries tend to have lower tax rates and thus unweighted averages are lower than weighted averages in most cases. In the results presented in this report, both weighted and unweighted averages are reported, but weighted averages are more relevant to making comparisons of measures of the tax burden on capital deployed around the world.

Tax Rate Comparisons: United States Compared with OECD and Large Economies

Table 1 reports the three measures of effective tax rates, with marginal rates restricted to equipment and structures separately, for the United States and the OECD excluding the United States. The statutory rate is reported with and without the production activities deduction.

Table 1. Corporate Tax Rates, United States and Rest of the OECD

Tax Rate Measure and Year	United States	OECD Excluding United States, GDP Weighted Average	OECD Excluding United States, Unweighted Average
Statutory (2010)	39.2	29.6	25.5
Statutory (2010) with Production Activities Deduction	36.3	29.6	25.5
Effective (2008)	27.1	27.7	23.3
Marginal Effective Equipment (2010)	23.6	21.2	17.3
Marginal Effective Equipment (2005)	23.0	21.1	18.7
Marginal Effective Buildings (2005)	29.0	26.4	23.4

Source: Statutory tax rates and gross domestic product (GDP), Organisation for Economic Co-operation and Development (OECD), http://www.oecd.org/dataoecd/26/56/33717459.xls and http://stats.oecd.org/Index.aspx? DatasetCode=SNA_TABLE1. Effective tax rate from Price WaterhouseCoopers, *Global Effective Tax Rate Comparisons—Methodology and Results*. Marginal tax rates, 2005, Institute for Fiscal Studies, http://www.ifs.org.uk/ publications/3210. Marginal tax rates 2010, Arparna Mathur and Kevin Hassett, *Report Card on Effective Corporate Tax Rates*, American Enterprise Institute, http://www.aei.org/outlook/101024. PriceWaterhouseCoopers reports similar effective tax rate data in their study Global Effective Tax Rates, April 14, 2011, at http://businessroundtable.org/uploads/studies-reports/downloads/Effective_Tax_Rate_Study.pdf.

The overall statutory rates in the OECD are slightly lower for 2013, with the rate in the OECD excluding the United States falling a little over a half to one percentage point. The U.S. rate is estimated at 39.1%, whereas the OECD weighted average is 28.4% and the unweighted average is 25.1%.[7] The weighted rate was influenced by rate reductions in Japan and the United Kingdom.

The marginal tax rates do not reflect the effect of the production activities deduction that likely applies to most multinational corporations and would decrease these tax rates by 2-3 percentage points as of 2010. (The deduction was 3% in 2005-2006 and 6% for 2007-2009.) Thus while the difference between the statutory rate and the simple average—a difference of 13.7 percentage points—is frequently reported, a difference of about half that much—or 6.6 percentage points— occurs when the adjusted statutory rate of 36.2% is compared with the weighted average of 29.6%. The effective tax rate (which would automatically capture the production activities deduction and other provisions) is about the same. The marginal effective rate rates are also about the same when adjusted. Thus the tax rate most relevant for the purpose of incentives to invest is similar for the United States and the rest of the OECD with respect to equipment and structures investment.

The marginal tax rates do not reflect the temporary bonus depreciation in effect for 2008-2010 in the United States, which allowed 50% of the cost of equipment to be deducted. A provision allowing 100% of the cost to be deducted is in place for 2011. Because these are temporary provisions, it seems appropriate to exclude them. Whether these measures are captured in the effective tax rate depends on the treatment of deferred taxes, but measures from different years appear similar.

The OECD excludes some large countries, such as China and Brazil. **Table 2** provides the statutory and effective tax rate comparisons for the 15 largest countries, which account for three-quarters of world gross domestic product (GDP). The results are similar to those in **Table 1** with the weighted average about 1 percentage point higher. With the production activities deduction the rates differ by 5.6 percentage points. The effective rate is the same.

Table 2. Corporate Tax Rates in the 15 Largest Countries

Tax Rate Measure and Year	United States	Remaining 14 Large Countries, GDP Weighted Average	Remaining 14 Large Countries, Unweighted Average
Statutory (2010)	39.2	30.7	29.8
Statutory (2010) Including Production Activities Deduction	36.3	30.7	29.8
Effective (2008)	27.1	27.2	25.3

Source: Statutory tax rates are at http://www.worldwide-tax.com/#partthree; effective tax rates are from same source as **Table 1**. GDP is from the World Bank http://siteresources.worldbank.org/DATASTATISTICS/ Resources/GDP.pdf.

Tax rates have declined slightly, to a weighted average of 30 and an unweighted average of 29.2.[8]

---

[7] Calculated from OECD data. Corporate rates at http://www.oecd.org/ctp/taxpolicyanalysis/ oecdtaxdatabase htm#C_CorporateCaptial; GDP at http://stats.oecd.org/Index.aspx?DataSetCode=SNA_TABLE1.

[8] Tax rates are at http://www kpmg.com/Global/en/services/Tax/tax-tools-and-resources/Pages/corporate-tax-rates-table.aspx.

Table 3, **Table 4**, and **Table 5** provide results for effective tax rates from other studies. **Table 3** reports the Markle and Shackleford study that estimates the effective tax rate of domestic firms in different countries. Because a smaller number of countries are examined, **Table 3** compares the U.S. rate with that of the six large countries.

Table 3. Effective Corporate Tax Rates, United States Compared with Six Countries

Tax Rate Measure	United States	Six Large Countries, GDP Weighted Average	Six Large Countries, Unweighted Average
Effective (2005-2009)	23.0	24.5	26.2

Source: Kevin S. Markle and Douglas A. Shackleford, "Cross-Country Comparisons of Corporate Income Taxes," working paper, February 2011.

Note: The six countries are Canada, France, Germany, India, Japan, and United Kingdom.

Table 4 and **Table 5** report the Swenson and Lee study that estimated effective rates for firms headquartered in various countries for 2006 and 2007. The tables report for 2006 pre-dated the start of the recession and do not include years with bonus depreciation. Both results confirm the findings of other studies: effective tax rates in the United States and in other countries are similar.

Table 4. Effective Tax Rates, United States and OECD

Tax Rate Measure	United States	OECD Excluding United States, GDP Weighted Average	OECD Excluding United States, Unweighted Average
Effective (2006)	29.5	28.4	23.7

Source: Charles Swenson and Namryoung Lee, "The Jury Is In: U.S. Companies are Overtaxed Relative to Their International Competitors," AICPA, July 17, 2008, at http://www.cpa2biz.com/Content/media/ PRODUCER_CONTENT/Newsletters/Articles_2008/Tax/juryin.jsp. Rate table at https://media.cpa2biz.com/ newsletter/2008/Tax/july/juryin_table.htm.

Table 5. Effective Tax Rates in the 15 Largest Countries

Tax Rate Measure	United States	Remaining 14 Large Countries, GDP Weighted Average	Remaining 14 Large Countries, Unweighted Average
Effective (2006)	29.5	28.7	27.3

Source: Charles Swenson and Namryoung Lee, "The Jury Is In: U.S. Companies are Overtaxed Relative to Their International Competitors, AICPA, July 17, 2008, at http://www.cpa2biz.com/Content/media/ PRODUCER_CONTENT/Newsletters/Articles_2008/Tax/juryin.jsp. Rate table at https://media.cpa2biz.com/ newsletter/2008/Tax/july/juryin_table.htm.

Table 6 returns to the estimates of marginal effective tax rates, and expands the marginal rate analysis to reflect the other categories of assets, inventories, and intangibles. It provides a weighted average of these tax rates, using data on capital stock shares from the United States but applying the same shares to other countries. Note that intangibles are generally taxed at negative tax rates both in the United States and abroad. Expenditures on research, advertising, and human capital investment are generally deducted when incurred, which leads to a zero effective tax rate, and most countries (including the United States) have additional subsidies or credits for research expenditures.

Table 6. Marginal Effective Tax Rates, United States and Weighted OECD

	U.S. Without Production Activities Deduction	U.S. With Production Activities Deduction	OECD Excluding United States, OECD, GDP Weighted	OECD Excluding United States, GDP Weighted, Adjusted by Statutory Rate Changes
Equipment	23.0	21.2	21.1	18.9
Structures	29.0	26.7	26.4	23.6
Inventories	39.2	36.2	29.6	29.6
Intangibles	-4.7	-4.7	-9.7	-9.7
Total	**22.2**	**20.2**	**18.3**	**16.4**

Source: Tax rates on equipment and structures from **Table 1**, Inventories taxed at statutory rates. Tax rates on intangibles, Department of Finance, Canada, *Tax Expenditures and Evaluations 2009 : Part 2, An International Comparison of Tax Assistance for Investment in Research and Development,* http://www.fin.gc.ca/taxexp-depfisc/2009/taxexp0902-eng.asp. Weights are 24.2% equipment, 39.6% structures, 9.7% inventories, and 26.5% intangibles. For intangibles, 49% arise from R&D, which is taxed at rates of -10.1% in the U.S, -22.2% in the weighted OECD average, and -54.2% in the simple OECD average. The remaining intangibles arising from human capital investment and advertising are taxed at a 0 rate. Data on corporate equipment, structures, and inventories for 2003 from Flow of Funds Accounts 1995-2004, p. 96, http://www.federalreserve.gov/Releases/Z1/Current/annuals/a1995-2004.pdf. Estimates of intangibles from Carol Corrado, Charles Hulten, and Daniel Sichel, *Intangible Capital and Economic Growth,* Finance and Economic Discussion Series, Division of Research and Statistics Federal Reserve Board, 2006-4, http://www.federalreserve.gov/releases/z1/20050921/z1.pdf.

As **Table 6** indicates, the overall marginal effective tax rates for the United States accounting for the production activities deduction and for the OECD countries weighted by GDP are similar, 20% and 18%. The differences are larger if the OECD rate is adjusted by average statutory rate changes that have occurred in these OECD countries since 2005, although base broadening could offset that reduction.[9] Marginal tax rates are also significantly lower than the statutory rates: the U.S. rate is about half the statutory rate and the weighted OECD rate is about 60% of the statutory rate.

The next measure is another marginal tax rate measure (Chen and Mintz). This measure has a number of differences from those in **Table 1** and **Table 4**. It includes equipment, structures, inventories, and land, but not intangibles. It also includes the effects of transfer taxes that fall on capital and debt finance. In the United States, these taxes are primarily state and local retail sales taxes that apply to capital goods purchases or inputs into construction and are quite large. It also includes franchise taxes. It does not, however, include wealth, capital stock, or property taxes. The measure also allows for debt finance and uses capital stock weights for Canada.

Table 7 reports these estimates for the OECD. Based on comments made in a previous analysis, indicating the size of these additional state and local taxes, the table reports a number with these additional taxes subtracted out to allow more comparability to other results. As compared with the numbers in **Table 6**, the discrepancy in the weighted OECD and the United States is larger. If the adjusted rates in **Table 6** are recomputed to exclude intangibles, they would be 28.7% for the

---

[9] Rate changes between 2005 and 2010 largely reflect the reduction in the German tax rate, although the U.K. rate also fell. However, these measures do not reflect changes in the base, which apparently provided some offsetting revenue. See Simon Kennedy, "Tax Cut War Widens in Europe," *New York Times,* May 28, 2997, http://www nytimes.com/2007/05/28/business/worldbusiness/28iht-tax.4.5899993 html?_r=1.

United States and 23% for the OECD (weighted). This differential of 5.7 points shrinks to 3.8 points when intangibles are included. The only other differential is that these rates should be lowered to reflect the effects of debt finance. Normally, higher statutory tax rates result in a larger negative tax rate on debt, so the United States rate should fall more for this reason (although this effect can vary with inflation).

The differential between the United State and the OECD as reported in the original study is 16.2 percentage points (34.6% minus 18.4%). Out of that differential, 5.2 points are due to using an unweighted average, 5.0 points are due to including transfer taxes, 1.9 points are due to excluding intangibles, and the remaining 4.1 points are similar to the difference found in **Table 6**.

Table 7. Marginal Tax Rates Including Transfer and Franchise Taxes, United States Compared with the OECD

Tax Rate Measure	United States	OECD Excluding United States, GDP Weighted Average	OECD Excluding United States, Unweighted Average
Average Marginal Tax Rate 2010	34.6	23.6	18.4
Average Marginal Tax Rate Correcting for Additional Taxes	27.6	21.6	16.4

Source: Duanjie Chen and Jack Mintz, "New Estimates of Effective Corporate Tax Rates on Business Investment," CATO Institute, *Tax and Budget Bulletin*, no. 64 , February 2011, http://www.cato.org/pubs/tbb/tbb_64.pdf. Indications that transfer taxes added 7 points for the United States and 2 points for other countries on average is from the previous year's tax rates, "U.S. Effective Corporate Tax Rate on New Investments: Highest in the OECD," May 2010.

An updated study for 2012 shows similar relationships. The United States tax rate was 35.6%, the OECD excluding the United States was 24.0% weighted and 19.6% unweighted.[10]

Table 8 reports the comparative rates for the 15 largest countries. These rates are closer together, and quite close when adjusted for transfer taxes.

Table 8. Marginal Effective Tax Rates Including Transfer Taxes, 15 Largest Countries

Tax Rate Measure	United States	Remaining Large 14 Countries, GDP Weighted Average	Remaining Large 14 Countries Excluding U.S. – Unweighted Average
Average Marginal Tax Rate 2010	34.6	26.3	27.0
Average Marginal Tax Rate Correcting for Additional State and Local Taxes	27.6	24.3	25.0

Source: Duanjie Chen and Jack Mintz, "New Estimates of Effective Corporate Tax Rates on Business Investment," CATO Institute, *Tax and Budget Bulletin*, no. 64 , February 2011, http://www.cato.org/pubs/tbb/tbb_64.pdf. Indications that transfer taxes added 7 points for the United States and 2 points for other countries

---

[10] Calculated from data in Duanjie Chen and Jack Mintz, "Corporate Tax Competitiveness Rankings for 2012," CATO Institute, *Tax and Budget Bulletin*, no. 65, September 2012, http://www.cato.org/sites/cato.org/files/pubs/pdf/tbb_65.pdf.

on average is from the previous year's tax rates, "U.S. Effective Corporate Tax Rate on New Investments: Highest in the OECD," May 2010.

The Chen and Mintz study makes an important point, namely that other taxes outside of the corporate tax can affect the relative burden of tax in a way that could affect investment. (These types of taxes would not be relevant for profit shifting.) The main reservation about this finding is that the inclusion of these other capital taxes is partial. The other main capital tax in the United States is the property tax, which probably adds another 3 percentage points to the rate, but other countries also have property taxes as well as wealth taxes.[11]

Table 9 reports a fourth type of tax rate measure, which is named by its developers the "effective average tax rate." Estimates using this method differentiate between a normal (or riskless) return, which is taxed at an effective rate that reflects the various tax benefits such as accelerated depreciation, and the excess return, which is taxed at the statutory rate. Thus, it is a mix of marginal tax rates and statutory tax rates. This measure is reported because it is available and cited by some researchers. Some evidence suggests that it is a better predictor of location than other measures.[12] It shows U.S. taxes to be significantly higher than OECD rates, but the implications of such a measure for economic behavior are not clear.

Economists sometimes, when examining investment subsidies, differentiate between the normal and excess return. The normal return's tax burden is affected by items such as accelerated depreciation and investment subsidies, whereas the excess profit is subject to the statutory rate. In these views, however, it is the tax on normal return that would, in any case, affect economic behavior. The excess return is generally seen as bearing little or no tax burden because the reduction in expected return due to tax is offset by the reduction in variance of after tax return (i.e., the tax reduces gains and losses).

One reason that a combination of statutory and effective marginal rates might have an effect on location is that firms may locate some physical activity in a country to facilitate profit shifting associated with setting up subsidiaries to exploit developed intangibles.[13]

---

[11] According to Jennifer Gravelle, "Empirical Essays on the Causes and Consequences of Tax Policy: A Look at Families, Labor, and Property" (Ph.D. diss., George Washington University, January 2008), the effective property tax rate, which applies almost solely to buildings, is 1.59%. Multiplying this rate by the share of buildings in the capital stock (39.6%) and by one minus the tax rate of 36.2%, because these taxes are deductible, results in an overall rate of 0.4%. Assuming a pre-tax equity return of 12%, it adds about 3 percentage points to the rate. For information on property and wealth taxes in the European Union, which can be quite significant in some countries, see the documents at http://ec.europa.eu/taxation_customs/taxation/gen_info/economic_analysis/tax_structures/index_en.htm.

[12] Michael Devereux and Rachel Griffith, "Taxes and the Location of Production: Evidence from a Panel of US Multinationals," *Journal of Public Economics*, vol. 68, June 1998, pp. 335-367.

[13] For example, newspaper reports have indicated that Google and Forest Labs set up sales and production facilities in Ireland as part of a measure that ultimately caused profits to be realized in Bermuda. See Jesse Drucker, "Google 2.4% Rate Shows How $60 Billion Lost to Tax Loopholes," *Bloomberg*, October 21, 2010, at http://www.bloomberg.com/news/2010-10-21/google-2-4-rate-shows-how-60-billion-u-s-revenue-lost-to-tax-loopholes.html and Jesse Drucker, "U.S. Companies Dodge $60 Billion in Taxes in Global Odyssey," *Bloomberg*, May 13, 2010, at http://www.bloomberg.com/news/2010-05-13/american-companies-dodge-60-billion-in-taxes-even-tea-party-would-condemn.htm.

Table 9. "Effective Average Tax Rate," United States and OECD

Tax Rate Measure	United States	Most OECD Excluding United States, GDP Weighted Average	Most OECD Excluding United States, Unweighted Average
Effective Average (2009)	37.4	29.8	24.3

Source: Michael P. Devereux, Christina Elschner, Dieter Endres, and Christoph Spengel, "Effective Tax Rates Using the Devereux-Griffith Methodlogy," ZEW Center for European Economic Research, October 2009, http://ec.europa.eu/taxation_customs/resources/documents/common/publications/studies/etr_company_tax.pdf. This research was focused on the European Union and selected additional countries; it excludes Australia, Chile, Iceland, New Zealand, Mexico, and Korea.

Summing Up

This comparison suggests some important precautions in comparing tax rates. First, it is important when forming a composite rate for the rest of the world to weight the tax rates by output or some other measure of economic importance. Because small countries tend to have lower rates than large ones, comparing rates using simple averages across countries exaggerates the differential between the United States and tax burdens elsewhere in the world. Second, weighted statutory tax rates differ but effective tax rates do not. Marginal effective tax rates have small differences. Third, in comparing the differences in statutory rates, the effect of the production activities deduction narrows the differential by close to half. Finally, although the role of subnational taxes outside of the corporate tax appears to be important for investment decisions, a full comparison has yet to be made. This analysis suggests that reform of state and local sales taxes could contribute to a more efficient system.

Economic Effects of a U.S. Rate Cut

The previous analysis has shown that U.S. statutory corporate tax rates are about 10 percentage points higher than a weighted average of the OECD or the large countries that account for most of output (7 percentage points when including the production activities deduction). Effective tax rates are about the same, and marginal effective tax rates are only slightly larger in the United States. The effects of including other capital taxes have not yet been explored on a comprehensive basis, although U.S. retail sales taxes on capital goods and franchise taxes are estimated to create an additional 5 percentage point differential.

This section explores the effects of a U.S. rate cut on the United States. The first subsection examines the effects on revenue, output, and national income for a corporate rate cut in isolation, only looking at capital flows. The second subsection discusses potential implications for profit shifting. The third subsection considers the possibility that other countries would react to a U.S. rate cut by cutting their rates as well. Finally, discussions of outlook for and consequences of a revenue neutral corporate tax reform are presented.

Effects on Revenue, Output, and National Welfare, Assuming No Tax Rate Changes by Other Countries or Offsetting Base Broadening in the United States

This section examines the effects of a corporate rate cut from 35% to 25% on revenues and international capital flows, and their effects on the U.S. economy (including feedback effects on revenues and effects on national welfare). It focuses on issues specific to global economy considerations of the corporate tax, not the traditional corporate tax issues that would also occur in a closed economy.

Revenues

The Congressional Budget Office (CBO) projected a 10-year corporate revenue of $4,360 billion from FY2013 to FY20221.[14] If this number were multiplied by 10/35 to estimate the revenue loss, the result would be $1,245 billion per year, on average.[15] The loss, however, is likely to be larger because net tax liability is the tax rate times taxable income, minus credits. Rate changes would not normally affect credits, and, if not, the revenue loss would be projected based on tax liability before credits. According to Internal Revenue Service (IRS) data, corporate tax before credits is 134% of corporate tax after credits.[16]

One of the major credits, the foreign tax credit, would be affected, in some cases, by a rate cut. The foreign tax credit is limited to the U.S. tax because of foreign source income, so as the U.S. rate falls, the limit on credits also falls. In some cases, the credit would not be affected, or not affected proportionally, because the foreign tax credits are less than the limit and a change in the limit would not necessarily change foreign tax credits. (These firms are termed excess limit firms.) In other cases, firms have creditable taxes above the limit; with credits equal to the limit, a reduction in the limit would reduce foreign tax credits proportionally. (These firms are termed excess credit firms.)

Tax liability after the foreign tax credit but before other credits (general business credits and the alternative minimum tax credit) is 105.7% of tax liability after all credits. If foreign tax credits are reduced proportionally, the average loss is almost $132 billion. If foreign tax credits are not affected at all, the average loss per year is $168 billion.[17]

These estimates suggest that over the 10-year period, $1.3 trillion to $1.7 trillion would be lost in revenues due to the proposed rate cut. This number does not include any behavioral feedback effects, which could reduce the cost, but also does not include debt service or crowding out of private capital, which would increase the cost.

---

[14] See Congressional Budget Office, *The Budget and Economic Outlook, Fiscal Years 2013-FY2022*, January 2013, p. 85, at http://www.cbo.gov/sites/default/files/cbofiles/attachments/01-31-2012_Outlook.pdf.

[15] For a roughly flat tax rate, the percentage reduction in revenues would be the same as the percentage reduction in rate, so multiplying by the ratio of the percentage point reduction, 10 percentage points, to the original rate, 35, provides an estimate of the revenue loss.

[16] Internal Revenue Service, Statistics of Income, Corporate Income Tax Returns for 2007, http://www.irs.gov/taxstats/article/0,,id=170726,00 html.

[17] The lower number multiplies $125 billion by 1.057 and the higher number multiplies $125 billion by 1.34.

Estimates implied by this calculation are larger than projections based on a percentage point rate increase contained in CBO's Budget Options which, applying the percentage loss to the new baseline suggests revenue losses of about $1,113 trillion.[18] Some part of the discrepancy may reflect the fact that liabilities lag collections and that the first full year does not apply because estimates are based on fiscal years. In addition, to the extent that firms have unused foreign credits, a rate increase would raise less than reduction of the same size would cost. Other behavioral effects may occur as well.

Regardless of the precise estimate, a revenue loss in excess of $1 trillion and in excess of $100 billion a year would be expected over the next 10 years.

Effects on U.S. Output and Wages

What about the effects on the U.S. economy? The discussion sometimes focuses on job creation. Job creation is an important issue for the government to address during cyclical downturns. Standard economic theory suggests such policies should be temporary; in contrast, advocates of corporate rate cuts are proposing permanent cuts. In any case, temporary or permanent corporate rate cuts are unlikely to be very effective stimulus policies.[19]

Economic theory suggests that there is no reason to view general job creation as a long-run objective of government policies. The economy can generate the jobs needed by the natural process of growth and market adjustment. In 1961 and 1991, the unemployment rate was the same, 6.7%. Employment, however, rose from 66 million to 117 million. Employment tends to grow steadily; the unemployment rate fluctuates. Long-term jobs policies, according to economic theory, therefore, should not be aimed at increasing jobs, although they can be designed to reduce structural or frictional unemployment (such as improving the skills of disadvantaged workers).[20]

Rather, the capital flows induced by a corporate rate cut generally have effects on the level of output and on wage levels, rather than the number of workers. Despite the claimed effects of cutting the corporate tax on encouraging the flow of foreign-owned capital into the country from abroad (inbound capital) or discouraging the flow of U.S. capital to other countries (outbound capital), there are many forces that constrain the movement of capital. As capital flows into a country, its greater abundance coupled with a fixed amount of labor drives the wage rate up and the rate of return down, so that the pre-tax return to capital falls. If the economy is large enough to affect the rest of the world's returns, the proportional flow of capital is lessened further,

---

[18] See Congressional Budget Office, *Reducing the Deficit: Spending and Revenue Options*, p. 173 at http://www.cbo.gov/sites/default/files/cbofiles/ftpdocs/120xx/doc12085/03-10-reducingthedeficit.pdf. The estimate for 2012-2021 was $100.6 billion while the baseline was $3.923 billion.

[19] Corporate rate cuts are not likely to be effective as a short-run stimulus. Several CRS Reports discuss the effectiveness of alternative tax provisions. See CRS Report R40104, *Economic Stimulus: Issues and Policies*, by Jane G. Gravelle, Thomas L. Hungerford, and Marc Labonte; CRS Report RS21136, *Government Spending or Tax Reduction: Which Might Add More Stimulus to the Economy?*, by Marc Labonte; CRS Report R41034, *Business Investment and Employment Tax Incentives to Stimulate the Economy*, by Thomas L. Hungerford and Jane G. Gravelle; CRS Report RS21126, *Tax Cuts and Economic Stimulus: How Effective Are the Alternatives?*, by Jane G. Gravelle; and CRS Report R41006, *Unemployment: Issues and Policies*, by Jane G. Gravelle, Thomas L. Hungerford, and Marc Labonte.

[20] If labor supply were responsive to wage increases, increased wages induced by capital flows could increase the size of the labor force, but evidence suggests that labor supply is relatively inelastic. See CRS Report RL31949, *Issues in Dynamic Revenue Estimating*, by Jane G. Gravelle, for a review of labor supply elasticity research.

---

because shift of capital from abroad (with no change in taxes) raises the after tax return abroad and draws some of the capital back. Capital flows are further reduced if there are significant non-corporate sectors (because a rate cut would draw capital from the unincorporated sectors of the economy as well as from abroad). Finally, the flow of capital would be further limited if capital is not perfectly mobile or products are not perfect substitutes.

A study by Gravelle and Smetters used a general equilibrium model to capture the effects of imposing a 35% tax, allowing for four sectors in the U.S. economy and a mirror foreign economy.[21] The estimated change in the capital stock, assuming the conditions most conducive to capital inflows, was 4.5%. (This scenario assumes that individuals and firms view investments in different locations as perfect substitutes and consumers view foreign and domestic products as perfect substitutes; these are referred to as the portfolio and product substitution elasticities and are set, effectively, at infinity.)[22] This effect implies a 4.7% increase from eliminating the tax (4.5/(1-4.5)). To convert a percentage change in the capital stock to a percentage change in output, multiply by the capital share of income, which was 0.29, to get a 1.36% increase in output. Because a partial change is proposed, multiply by 10/35 to obtain an estimated percentage change in output of 0.39%. With constant factor shares, which are assumed in this model, wages will also increase by this percentage.[23]

A similar magnitude of effects can be obtained by examining revenue reductions and incidence estimates for this same perfectly mobile case. CBO projects the corporate tax at 2% of GDP.[24] This revenue is as a percentage of gross output (which includes output that replaces capital and thus is not a part of an income concept). To convert it to a percentage of net of depreciation output (which is 82% of gross output[25]), divide by 0.82, for corporate revenues that are 2.27% of domestically generated income. To capture the effect of reducing the tax by 10 percentage points, multiply by 10/35, to obtain a tax cut of 0.65% of income. Incidence studies indicate that about 73% of the burden of the corporate tax falls on labor under this perfectly mobile assumption,[26] so

---

[21] Jane G. Gravelle and Kent A. Smetters, "Does the Open Economy Assumption Really Mean That Labor Bears the Burden of a Capital Income Tax?" *Advances in Economic Analysis and Policy*, vol. 6, iss. 1, 2006, pp. 1-40. Results of simulations are on p. 25.

[22] An elasticity is the percentage change in quantity divided by percentage change in price and a substitution elasticity is the percentage change in the ratio of two quantities divided by the percentage change in the ratios of their prices. For the portfolio elasticity the ratio is between domestic and foreign assets relating to their relative after tax returns, while for the product substitution elasticity it is the ratio of the domestic and imported traded good as it relates to the relative prices. Other elasticities also appear in the model, which are generally set at 1; these include substitution between factors of production and products produced by the different sectors.

[23] This correlation requires a Cobb-Douglas production function, which has a unitary factor substitution elasticity.

[24] Congressional Budget Office, *The Budget and Economic Outlook, Fiscal Years 2012-FY2021*, January 2011, p. 87. http://www.cbo.gov/ftpdocs/120xx/doc12039/01-26_FY2011Outlook.pdf.

[25] *Economic Report of the President*, February 2010, p. 360, data are for 2006, the year before the recession began.

[26] This finding was reported by William Randolph, *International Burdens of the Corporate Income Tax*, Congressional Budget Office, Working Paper 2006-09, August 2006, http://www.cbo.gov/ftpdocs/75xx/doc7503/2006-09.pdf as well as by Jane G. Gravelle and Kent A. Smetters, "Does the Open Economy Assumption Really Mean That Labor Bears the Burden of a Capital Income Tax?" *Advances in Economic Analysis and Policy*, vol. 6, iss. 1, pp. 1-40. An earlier general equilibrium study found 84% of the burden fell on labor under these circumstances: John Mutti and Harry Grubert, "The Taxation of Capital Income in an Open Economy: The Importance of Resident-Nonresident Tax Treatment," *Journal of Public Economics* 27 (August 1985): 291-309. Their study assumes a production function with a much lower elasticity, so that the change in wage rate would be much larger than the change in overall output. This type of function allows a smaller percentage change in the capital stock to have a larger effect on labor income. Although their effects on wages are larger, their effects on capital inflows and total output are smaller. Another study sometimes mentioned is Arnold C. Harberger. Harberger's paper, "Corporate Tax Incidence: Reflections on What is (continued...)

---

this number is multiplied by 0.73 to obtain an increase in labor income of 0.47% of total income. Based on national income accounts, the share of labor income is 76%,[27] so dividing 0.47 by 0.76 yields a 0.62% increase in output and in wages.

Both estimates suggest a relatively small effect on output, of around 0.5%, but this estimate is too large. Perfect product substitution is not possible in a multi-good economy.[28] Moreover, empirical evidence suggests elasticities that are smaller. Gravelle and Smetters propose as a more reasonable case a model with portfolio and product substitution elasticities of 3. This assumption yields a 1.6% change in the capital stock. Following the methodology outlined above, the effect on output and wages is 0.13%, rather than 0.4%. These elasticities reduce the share of the burden borne by labor to 21% and, again, following the same methodology would cause an output and wage effect of about 0.18% rather than 0.62%.[29]

Two other aspects might make these effects even lower or perhaps reverse the sign. First, the effect of debt capital is not incorporated into any of these models. Because about a third of the capital stock is financed by debt, the magnitude of the first set of estimates (using capital stock estimates) should be reduced by about one-third to account for the presence of debt. This would be the expected outcome if returns to debt-financed investment were taxed at a zero rate, as would be the case if there were no inflation and no accelerated depreciation. However, since both of these conditions exist in the U.S. tax code, debt is subsidized at the corporate level because inflation is generally positive and the effective marginal tax rate is below the statutory rate. Lowering the statutory rate reduces these subsidies and discourages debt. This effect may be desirable for issues such as the debt-equity distortion, but can actually discourage capital inflows, as suggested in one study.[30]

(...continued)

Known, Unknown, and Unknowable," in John W. Diamond and George R. Zodrow, eds., *Fundamental Tax Reform: Issues, Choices, and Implications* (Cambridge, Mass.: MIT Press, 2008). That paper reports 130% of the tax falling on labor income, but the analysis is not really a model of the U.S. economy calibrated to observed values, but an illustration. The illustration assumes a much higher capital intensity in the corporate traded sector relative to the economy as whole than evidence suggests. For a discussion of these four models and their underlying differences, see Jennifer Gravelle, *Corporate Tax Incidence: Review of General Equilibrium Estimates and Analysis*, Congressional Budget Office, Working Paper 2010-03, May 2010, http://www.cbo.gov/ftpdocs/115xx/doc11519/05-2010-Working_Paper-Corp_Tax_Incidence-Review_of_Gen_Eq_Estimates.pdf.

[27] *Economic Report of the President*, February 2010, p. 362, data are for 2006, the year before the recession began. The share is calculated as the sum of compensation of employees plus 75% of proprietor's income, divided by the sum of compensation of employees, proprietor's income, corporate profits, rental income and interest income.

[28] In economics parlance, the result would be a corner solution where a country produces only one, or a few traded goods.

[29] The only other study that examines lower elasticities is that of John Mutti and Harry Grubert, "The Taxation of Capital Income in an Open Economy: The Importance of Resident-Nonresident Tax Treatment," *Journal of Public Economics* 27 (August 1985): 291-309. Their study still finds a large share of the burden falling on labor, but assumes a very low factor substitution elasticity that dominates the outcome and also makes it not possible to generalize about output effects from their incidence results. For a discussion of the role of the factor substitution elasticity as well as a review of the literature on elasticities, see Jennifer Gravelle, *Corporate Tax Incidence: Review of General Equilibrium Estimates and Analysis*, Congressional Budget Office, Working Paper 2010-03, May 2010, http://www.cbo.gov/ftpdocs/115xx/doc11519/05-2010-Working_Paper-Corp_Tax_Incidence-Review_of_Gen_Eq_Estimates.pdf. This paper finds the portfolio and product substitution elasticities of 3 to be consistent with the evidence but suggests that the factor substitution elasticity should be somewhat lower, leading to a share of the tax falling on labor of around 40% but a smaller capital flow and a smaller total change in output.

[30] Harry Grubert and John Mutti, "International Aspects of Corporate Tax Integration: The Role of Debt and Equity Flows," *National Tax Journal*, vol. 47, March, 1994, pp. 111-133.

Second, the estimates of capital stock assume that the United States has a territorial tax (i.e., the only tax due is on domestic profits). Although a relatively small share of foreign source income is taxed, the U.S. system is not fully territorial, but rather defers the tax until income is repatriated (except for branch income and some passive income that is easily shifted).[31] Under the U.S. system, the tax on income that is repatriated or currently taxed can be partially or fully offset by credits for foreign taxes paid. Most foreign source income is not taxed either because it is not repatriated or because credits are used to offset the tax; in addition to credits for tax paid in a country, unused credits from countries with higher taxes than the United States can be used to offset tax on income repatriated from low tax countries (called cross crediting).[32]

Effects on National Income and National Welfare

Even though output (or domestically generated income) increases by small amounts, that output gain does not represent a gain in U.S.-worldwide income. The gains that labor experiences are offset by the losses in the pre-tax return by the existing domestic capital, reducing the benefits of these firms. For example, in the case where labor income increases by 21% of the tax, existing capital, which absent capital flows would have had income increase by 100% of the tax cut, now has that increase offset roughly by 21% of the tax due to the lower pretax return. Although both labor and capital have higher after tax income, there is a transfer between the government and individuals, which must be offset by other tax increases or reduced spending either now or in the future.

Although there will be some gains in national welfare, they are likely to be only a small fraction of the revenue change. They would arise from income that transfers from foreigners to U.S. persons.[33] For thinking about this effect, consider separately inbound capital (capital owned by foreigners and invested in the United States) and outbound capital (capital owned by U.S. persons and invested abroad). The increase in inbound capital generates returns, but those returns are the income of the foreign investors. Thus, the only gain for the United States is the change in taxes, and the lower pre-tax rate of return on inbound investment. For outbound capital, the returns already belong to U.S. firms, and the gain is from moving capital back into the United States where taxes formerly paid to foreign governments are paid to the United States.

A recent study examined these effects, using data on foreign and domestic tax rates from a 2008 GAO study and estimates of inbound and outbound capital from the National Income and Product Accounts and found modest effects.[34] The estimated output effects in this study were larger than

---

[31] If dividends are eventually to be taxed, then there is no obvious benefit to deferral because the income will either be taxed currently or taxed with interest in the future (and the present value of the tax will be the same). However, some income can be indefinitely deferred in the steady state to allow for growth, firms have developed techniques for repatriating without paying tax, and firms can use excess foreign tax credits from high tax countries to shield income from tax.

[32] The residual tax rate on foreign subsidiaries of U.S. parents is 4%. See U.S. Government Accountability Office, *U.S. Multinational Corporations: Effective Tax Rates are Correlated With Where Income is Reported*, GAO-08-950, 2008.

[33] To the extent that taxes in the United States are higher than elsewhere, there could be efficiency gains as well, although Gravelle and Smetters find these to be small. They find an efficiency gain of 3% of revenue for eliminating the tax entirely. Because the excess burden rises with the square of the tax rate, about half the gain, 1.5% of revenue, would occur with the first 10 percentage points. However, this gain accrues to the world (and the United States would presumably get only a share equal to its share of world GDP, or about one-half of a percent of revenue) and is measured assuming there are no other taxes. Given other countries have similar tax rates, the effect could disappear entirely or be negative. But in any case, it is small enough to be disregarded.

[34] Jane G. Gravelle, "International Tax Policy: Are We Heading in the Right Direction?," December 2010, Forthcoming (continued...)

---

those calculated above because the study used a partial equilibrium framework with a simplified single sector model designed to distinguish between outbound and inbound capital flows. The purpose, however, was to consider the general magnitude of welfare effects. The estimates found that there was a slight *loss* (3% of the additional output) for inbound capital because the reduction in the tax rate on existing capital inflows was less than fully offset by taxes on induced capital flows and the small reduction in pre-tax returns. For outbound capital, the main source of increased capital, there was a gain of 12% of output because taxes on this capital were paid to the United States rather than foreign governments. Overall, only about 9% of the output increase was a benefit to the United States which, for the magnitude of effects calculated, is less than two-hundredth of 1% of output and less than 3% of revenue.

These findings are quite consistent with optimal tax theories. For inbound capital, the optimal tax rate should be $1/(1+e)$ where e is the elasticity of the flow of inbound capital.[35] Because the study used an estimated effective tax rate of 25% and the optimal tax rate is 25% when e is 3, a negligible effect on welfare would be expected. For outbound capital, the optimality rule is to tax foreign source income net of foreign taxes for a small country, with a slightly higher rate on outbound capital returns for a large country.[36] Because current tax rules impose taxes much smaller than this rate and cause too much capital to be allocated abroad, cutting the U.S. tax rate improves welfare. However, the effects are small compared with either the U.S. economy or revenue.[37]

Revenue Feedback Effects

A final issue is the magnitude of revenue feedbacks from the output increase. Recall that the corporate tax cut discussed is about 0.65% of net output.

This increase in output is taxed with a mix of both labor and capital taxes. The marginal tax rate on labor income is estimated by CBO at 28.4% and the capital income tax rate is estimated at 11.5%.[38] The 11.5% is further reduced by 2 percentage points to account for the reduction in the corporate rate, to 9.5%. The overall marginal tax rate is 23.7%. Multiplying the 0.13% and the 0.18% increases in output by 23.7% yields an offset of 4.7% to 6.6%. (If infinite elasticities were

---

(...continued)

in the Proceedings of the National Tax Association.

[35] This result is derived by maximizing the benefit to inbound capital K: $F(K) - r(1-t)K$ with respect to t, the U.S. tax rate, where $F(K)$ is a production function and recognizing that r and K are functions of t and r is the marginal product of capital.

[36] This optimality rule maximizes the benefit to outbound capital, K, with respect to the foreign tax rate ($F(K) + r(1-t_f)K$, where t_f is the foreign tax rate.

[37] As mentioned earlier, this study focuses on the income effects of international capital flows. Reductions in the corporate tax rate could produce welfare gains, largely through reduction in the debt-equity distortion and changes in the composition of consumption, effects that would occur in a closed economy. In CRS Report RL34229, *Corporate Tax Reform: Issues for Congress*, by Jane G. Gravelle, these costs are estimated at about 10% to 15% of the corporate tax. Based on revenues of 2% of GDP and the rule of thumb that the excess burden rises with the square of the tax rate, the gain would be 0.1% to 0.15% of output from 10 percentage point rate reduction. These welfare tradeoffs do not rely on global economy considerations, and would largely not be experienced by an increase in income, but rather a decrease in risk and a more optimal composition of consumption.

[38] The rates are for 2009, which better reflect current tax rates. See Congressional Budget Office, *Analysis of the President's Budget*, March 2010, Tables 2.2 and 2.3, at http://www.cbo.gov/ftpdocs/112xx/doc11280/03-24-APB.pdf.

---

assumed and the output effects of 0.4% and 0.62% were considered the feedback effects would be from 14% to 23% of revenue.)

There are three reasons this feedback effect is probably too large (aside from the reservations about output effects due to debt finance discussed above). First, this tax on labor income does not account for the expectation that increases in labor income might be partially received through tax exempt employee fringe benefits or partially spent on tax favored purchases (such as charitable contributions). Second, absent other changes the share of individual taxes collected as payroll taxes would eventually lead to increased outlays for Social Security. Finally, the transition to the new capital stock will not be immediate.

In all the scenarios, these revenue offsets from behavioral changes would likely be smaller than the increase in revenue due to debt service, which is estimated at 25% on average over the 10-year period. In addition, if the increase in the debt displaces the capital stock, output would be reduced by 2021 enough to reduce revenues by 15% to 23% of the static cost. If revenues are not offset, and the increased debt crowds out the U.S. capital stock, output would be reduced about, 0.4% by 2021, an effect more than twice as large as the effects estimated from international capital inflows.[39]

Profit Shifting and Revenue Effects

Another aspect of behavior that is of concern for revenue is the possibility of profit shifting. It is more difficult to judge this effect. Because the evidence discussed above suggests that the revenue offset from corporate rate changes due to investment flows is likely in the neighborhood of 5%, real output effects do not appear large enough to make a corporate rate cut pay for itself in increased revenues, as some advocates claim.

Before examining profit shifting directly, consider the evidence cited to support the argument that there is a significant revenue shift. First, proponents point to studies that indicate a "Laffer curve" with a revenue maximizing tax rate of around 30%, using cross country panel data. These four studies were reviewed in a CRS report that found, due to both interpretation of the studies by proponents and statistical problems, these studies did not appear to support a gain in revenue from a cut in the U.S. tax rate.[40]

Proponents also make the general argument that the United States collects a smaller share of revenue relative to GDP than other countries, even though its rate is higher. For example, Hassett points out that the U.S. corporate revenue is 2% of GDP whereas the revenue of most other

---

[39] This calculation uses the 2021 GDP of $24 trillion projected by 2021 and assumes capital is 3.5 times output, for a total capital stock of $84 trillion. The cumulative revenue loss of $1.2 trillion is 1.4% of this capital stock, and multiplied by 0.3 would reduce output by 0.42%. Multiplied by the tax rates of 0.237 and divided by the static loss of 0.65% indicates an increase in the revenue loss of 15%. Using the $1.5 trillion estimate, the calculation yields an additional revenue loss of 20% and adding debt service net of the feedback effects from capital inflows yields 23%. Projected GDP is from CBO data at http://www.cbo.gov/ftpdocs/120xx/doc12039/Year-by-YearForecast_110125 xls.

[40] See CRS Report RL34229, *Corporate Tax Reform: Issues for Congress*, by Jane G. Gravelle. All of the studies were had methodological deficiencies due to lack of country fixed effects. One study did not find statistically significant effects in any case. The most sophisticated study actually found a much higher rate of 57% for a country like the United States. That study and another study were re-estimated using fixed effects and the statistical significant disappeared. This final study had an extremely short panel.

countries is 3%, and that the share has grown in some countries as rates have decreased.[41] Two factors other than profit shifting affect corporate revenues and their changes as a percent of GDP, the size of the base and the share of business income (and income in general) that is corporate source. Data shown earlier indicates that although the statutory rate is higher in the United States, the effective rate is not. Revenues patterns over time will reflect a combination of rate changes and base changes, and some countries financed some or all of their recent rate reductions with base broadening.[42] In addition, the size of the corporate sector will be affected by the ability of firms to operate in noncorporate form. A 2007 study by the U.S. Department of Treasury indicates that the U.S. rules allowing large firms to operate in noncorporate form are more generous than those of other countries. It also documented that the share of business income received by corporations in the United States had declined from 80% to 50% as more generous limits of the number of shareholders small corporations could have to elect taxation as unincorporated businesses were adopted and special forms of business such a limited liability corporations, taxed as partnerships, grew.[43] A recent OECD study indicated that corporate tax revenues, in addition to offsetting base changes, were increased by incentives to operate firms in corporate form and additional compliance measures.[44]

It is possible to consider the effect of profit shifting by examining direct estimates of the cost of profit shifting. These estimates of profit shifting suggest that they amount to 14% to 20% of total corporate tax revenue, which would not be enough to offset the revenue loss even if profit shifting disappeared entirely.[45] How much of a reduction in profit shifting might reasonably be expected? Because the profit shifting clearly occurs to the very low tax rate countries,[46] even a cut to 25% would leave a large benefit to profit shifting (it would lead to a combined federal and state rate of 29.8%, and 27.7% for eligible firms if the production activities deduction were retained). Recent discussions of a plan referred to as the double-Irish, Dutch sandwich showed two companies that, having moved profits to Ireland (with a 12.5% rate), took further steps to shift profits to Bermuda (with a 0% rate).[47] Because the cost in most cases is small, most firms would

---

[41] See Kevin Hassett, "Laffer Curve Pays Billions If Obama Just Asks," *Bloomberg Business Week*, February, 13, 2011, http://www.businessweek.com/news/2011-02-13/laffer-curve-pays-billions-if-obama-just-asks-kevin-hassett.html.

[42] See Steven Matthews, "Tax Reform: An International Perspective," Power Point presentation at the American Enterprise Institute, February 25, 2011, http://www.aei.org/docLib/MatthewsTaxReform.pdf.

[43] United States Department of the Treasury, "Treasury Tax Conference on Business Taxation and Global Competitiveness: Background Paper," July 30, 2007, at http://www.ustreas.gov/press/releases/hp500.htm.

[44] OECD, *Tax Policy Reform and Economic Growth*, OECD Publishing, 2010, http://dx.doi.org/10.1787/9789264091085-en.

[45] For reviews of profit shifting, see CRS Report R40623, *Tax Havens: International Tax Avoidance and Evasion*, by Jane G. Gravelle. The estimates used include those of Christian and Schultz of $30 billion compared with corporate revenues of $151 billion in 2001, those of Sullivan of $26 billion compared with revenues of $187 billion, and those of Clausing and Avi-Yonah of $60 billion compared with revenues of $370 billion. Corporate revenue numbers are from CBO, http://www.cbo.gov/ftpdocs/120xx/doc12039/HistoricalTables[1].pdf. Because the rate cut reduces revenues by 31% to 38%, the offset is less than 100% even if all profit shifting ended. A more recent estimate by Clausing indicates a loss of 20% to 30% depending on the method used. See Kimberly A. Clausing, "The Revenue Effects of Multinational Firm Income Shifting," *Tax Notes*, March 28, 20011, pp. 1581-1586.

[46] See, for example, Government Accountability Office, *U.S. Multinational Corporations: Effective Tax Rates are Correlated With Where Income is Reported*, GAO-08-950, August 2008. Other evidence is discussed in CRS Report R40623, *Tax Havens: International Tax Avoidance and Evasion*, by Jane G. Gravelle.

[47] See Jesse Drucker, "Google 2.4% Rate Shows How $60 Billion Lost to Tax Loopholes," *Bloomberg*, October 21, 2010, at http://www.bloomberg.com/news/2010-10-21/google-2-4-rate-shows-how-60-billion-u-s-revenue-lost-to-tax-loopholes.html and Jesse Drucker, "U.S. Companies Dodge $60 Billion in Taxes in Global Odyssey," *Bloomberg*, May 13, 2010, at http://www.bloomberg.com/news/2010-05-13/american-companies-dodge-60-billion-in-taxes-even-tea-party-would-condemn.htm.

probably continue to shift profits to the limit currently allowed by law as interpreted by the courts, and probably considerably less than proportionally to the tax rate change.

As discussed below, reforms to the tax treatment of foreign source income, by eliminating deferral and by restricting the foreign tax credit, or by focusing on limiting profit shifting techniques, might reduce the ability or benefits of profit-shifting and raise revenues.

Other Countries' Reactions to a U.S. Rate Reduction

An important policy issue for the United States is whether other countries might react to a U.S. rate reduction. Evidence shows that the initial cut in corporate tax rates around the world may have been triggered by the cut in the U.S. corporate tax rate from 48% to 35% from 1986 to 1988 as a result of the Tax Reform Act of 1986. **Figure 1** shows the statutory tax rates, beginning in 1981, for the United States and for the remainder of the OECD. The U.S. combined state and federal tax rate was about 50% and fell to just below 40% over those two years. Except for a slight rise in 1993, the tax rate has remained constant ever since. Two OECD numbers are provided: the unweighted numbers varying with the admission of new OECD members as well as tax rates and the GDP weighted tax rates of the OECD nations (outside the United States) in 1981. (Tax rates are shown in the **Appendix**, and they also indicate that the weighted average holding member country constant is about a percentage point higher.)

The tax rates for 2012 are similar to those for 2010: the unweighted average fell slightly from 25.5 to 24.9, but the weighted average was slightly higher, 29.8 compared to 29.6. The U.S. rate fell from 39.2% to 39.1%.[48]

While the simple (unweighted) average, which includes new entrants to the OECD, suggests a relatively continuous decline in rates, the weighted average indicates a more discrete pattern of tax cuts. As indicated by the graph, tax rates on average were close together before 1987 but rates of other countries began dropping in the next few years. For the weighted OECD average, the first drop followed the U.S. tax cut, but subsequently, rates were relatively constant over the next several years (and still slightly above U.S. rates). Tax rates then fell again, but stabilized around 2002 and were relatively unchanged until 2007, when Germany began cutting its tax rate. The fall beginning in the late 1990s may have been associated with the lower tax rates of the emerging former eastern bloc countries.

If one country cuts its tax rate, it attracts capital from other countries, which benefits labor and possibly overall national welfare, at the expense of other countries, as discussed above. However, if all countries cut their tax rates, none will gain capital but all will lose revenue. The observation of rate cuts in the rest of the world in the wake of the U.S. tax cut is not proof that countries will cut their rates again if the United States does, but it does provide some support for that expectation.

---

[48] Calculated from OECD data. Corporate rates at http://www.oecd.org/ctp/taxpolicyanalysis/ oecdtaxdatabase htm#C_CorporateCaptial; GDP at http://stats.oecd.org/Index.aspx?DataSetCode=SNA_TABLE1.

Figure 1. Statutory Tax Rates, United States and OECD (Excluding United States), 1981-2010

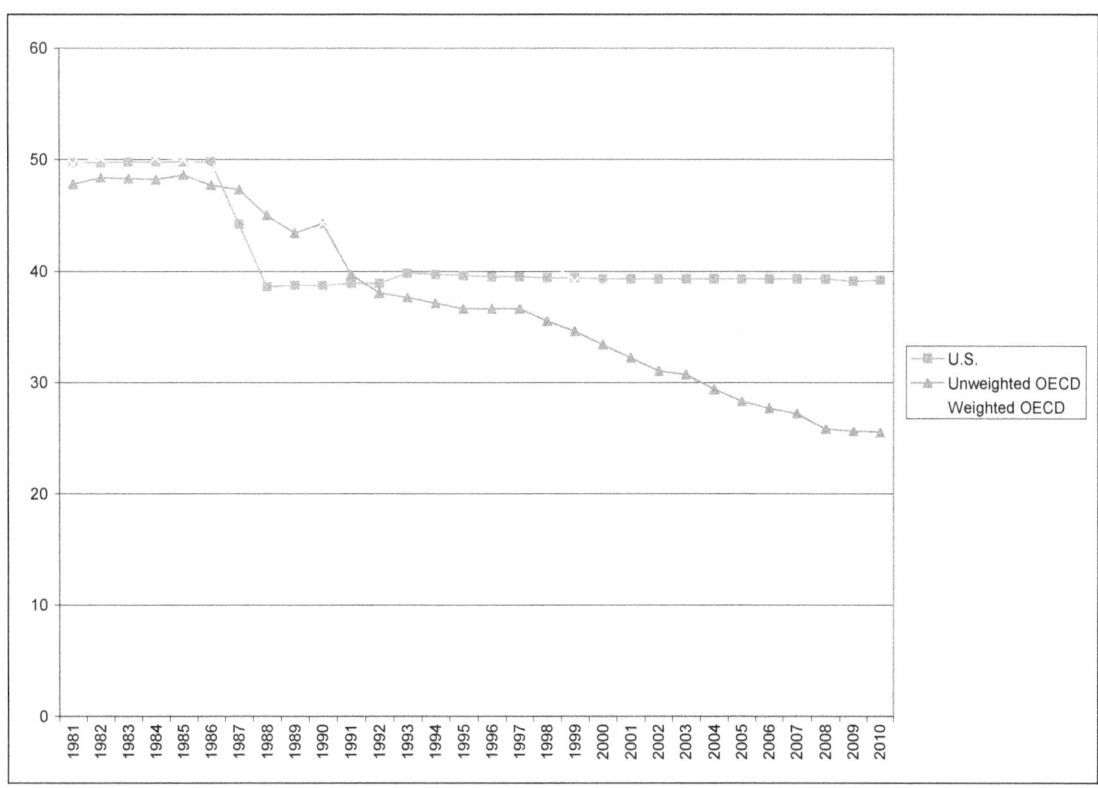

Source: CRS calculations based on tax rate data and GDP from the Organisation for Economic Co-operation and Development.

Notes: The weighted OECD measure provides for a constant set of initial countries, although this measure is only slightly different from that which covers all OECD countries with information available at any time. The unweighted measure includes the OECD countries in that year.

It is also possible that a smaller rate cut that does not move the United States to rates below those of other large countries would be less likely to trigger a response. For 2010, statutory tax rates for the next two largest countries in the remaining OECD, Japan and Germany, were 39.54% and 30.18% respectively, although Japan is proposing a 5 percentage point rate cut. The United Kingdom and France are respectively 28% and 34.4%, although the United Kingdom is planning further cuts to 24%. If the United States cut its federal rate to 25% its rate would be 29.8%; with the production activities deduction it would be 27.7%. A rate cut to 30% would result in a 34.5% rate (32% with the production activities deduction).[49] That rate would be similar to the rates in France, Japan, and Germany.

---

[49] Calculations are made by dividing revenues by an estimate of corporate taxes adjusting for the credits, so the revenue base of $3,293 billion for FY2012-FY2021 is increased to $4,728 billion. This number divides corporate revenues by the ratio of $112 billion to $135 billion per year, which relates the estimate of the rate cut without considering the effects of credits to the midpoint between allowing foreign tax credits and not allowing them (recall those estimates were $120 billion and $150 billion on average).

Revenue-Neutral Rate Reduction and Corporate Reform

If revenue concerns require offsetting corporate base broadening, what changes might be made and what are the consequences for international capital flows and profit shifting? This section discusses base broadening options, focusing on the largest corporate tax expenditures. The base broadening provisions are listed in **Table 10**, along with the reduction in the corporate rate the revenue change would allow for. Note that while each proposal is stated in terms of the rate reduction its revision would permit, the rate reductions for several provisions taken together are slightly smaller than the sum of their individual rate reductions because the progressively lower rates make base broadening less valuable.

Table 10. Rate Reduction Permitted by Certain Options, 2016

Possible Change in Provision	Percentage Point Reduction in Corporate Tax Rate
Accelerated Depreciation for Equipment (steady state)	3.0
Accelerated Deprecation for Equipment (steady state, corporate revenue gain only)	2.2
Production Activities Deduction	0.7
Taxation of Foreign Source Income	
—End Deferral	3.1
—End Deferral Plus Per Country Foreign Tax Credit Limit	4.0
—President Obama's Proposals	0.9
—Territorial Tax with Deduction Allocation	0.5
LIFO and Lower of Cost or Market Inventory Accounting	0.7
Deferral of Gain on non-Dealer Installment Sales	0.4
Deferral of Gain on Like-Kind Exchanges	0.4
Expensing of Research and Experimental Expenditures	0.4
Low Income Housing Credit	0.4
Subsidies for Fossil Fuels	0.1
Graduated Rates for Corporations	0.2
Insurance Subsidies	0.1
Credit Union Exemption	0.1
Eliminate all Corporate Tax Expenditures	7.9
Eliminate Corporate Tax Expenditures Except for International Provisions	5.5
Disallow Deduction for Inflation Portion of Interest	1.1
Shifting Into Corporate Form[a]	2.3
Rolling Back 2003 Rates for Dividends and Capital Gains[b]	4.0

Source: CRS calculations, see CRS Report R41743, *International Corporate Tax Rate Comparisons and Policy Implications*, by Jane G. Gravelle, for a further discussion including estimation of the last two provisions in Table 15. The new tax rate is calculated by dividing the current rate (35%) by (1+the revenue gain divided by corporate tax revenue). Corporate tax revenue projections are from Congressional Budget Office (CBO), The Budget and Economic Outlook: Fiscal Years 2013 to 2023, February 5, 2013, at http://www.cbo.gov/publication/43907. The corporate base was increased by 20% to account for revenue prior to tax credits. Data on most tax expenditures are from Joint Committee on Taxation, Estimates of Federal Tax Expenditures For Fiscal Years 2012-2017, JCS-1-13. February 1, 2013, at https://www.jct.gov/publications.html?func=startdown&id=4503. The title passage rule estimate Estimates of accelerated depreciation cannot be taken from the tax expenditure estimates because they are affected by bonus depreciation. These estimates are from a Joint Committee on Taxation memorandum from Thomas Barthold, Revenue Estimates, October 27, 2011, updated and multiplied by 2/3 to adjust from the budget horizon to the steady state as indicated by James B. Mackie III and John Kitchen "Slowing Depreciation in Corporate Tax Reform," *Tax Notes*, April 29, 2013, pp. 511-521. Estimates for deferral plus foreign tax credit limit and for the interest deduction were from Joint Committee on Taxation, 2010b Estimates of the Revenue Effect of S. 3018, The Bipartisan Simplification Act of 2010, November 2, 2010, at http://wyden.senate.gov/imo/media/doc/Score.pdf. Estimates for President Obama's proposals were from U.S. Department of the Treasury, General Explanations of the Administration's Fiscal Year 2012 Revenue Proposals, April, 2013, http://www.treasury.gov/resource-center/tax-policy/Documents/General-Explanations-FY2014.pdf . Estimates for the territorial tax were adapted from estimates in CBO, Reducing the Deficit: Spending and Revenue Options, March 10, 2011, p. 187, at http://www.cbo.gov/sites/default/files/cbofiles/ftpdocs/120xx/doc12085/03-10-reducingthedeficit.pdf.

Notes: These provisions are all estimated beginning at a 35% corporate rate and the sum would be larger than the combined effect. If evaluated at the lower rate the reduction would fall proportionally for most base broadening provisions, so the reduction would be 86% as large (.30/.35) if evaluated at a 30% rate. Note that these tax expenditures do not include temporary provisions, the most important of which are the research credit and the deferral of active financing income.

a. Assumes income distributed as in the early 1980s, a starting corporate rate of 30% and an individual rate of 30%. See text of CRS Report R41743, *International Corporate Tax Rate Comparisons and Policy Implications*, for other calculations.

b. Assumes a lower realization elasticity consistent with more recent evidence. With elasticity currently in use by the Treasury Department, the reduction would be 2.3 percentage points.

Accelerated Depreciation

Of the items listed among corporate tax expenditures, the single largest provision outside of deferral, is accelerated depreciation for equipment which, abstracting from the effect of temporary bonus depreciation, would allow a rate reduction of about 2 percentage points.[50] This measure is based on an alternative depreciation system. (Much more revenue would be raised in the short run, but revenue neutrality based on a 10-year budget window would lead to a long-run loss, because slowing depreciation leads to much larger revenue gains in the short run compared with the long run.) Equipment, in particular, is taxed at rates well below the statutory rate, at least at current inflation rates. Nevertheless, the desirability of restricting depreciation is unclear. A revenue neutral revision that cuts the rate in exchange for higher taxation of new investment would raise the marginal effective tax rate, because the rate reduction would apply to the return to existing capital. Moreover, estimates suggest that the value of depreciation under the alternative system would be too small and would tax investments at effective rates in excess of the statutory rates.[51] This provision would also raise revenues on unincorporated businesses, equivalent to about 30% of the corporate loss, which would permit a larger corporate rate reduction, by 3.3 percentage points.

---

[50] Estimates of depreciation as a percentage of revenues are from Jane G. Gravelle, "Practical Tax Reform for a More Efficient System, *Virginia Tax Review*," vol. 30, fall 2010, pp. 389-406.

[51] See Jane G. Gravelle, "Reducing Depreciation Allowances to Finance a Lower Corporate Tax Rate," National Tax Journal, vol. 64, December 2011, pp. 1039-1053; "Practical Tax Reform for a More Efficient System, *Virginia Tax Review*," vol. 30, fall 2010 , pp. 389-406;. Statement Before the Senate Committee on Finance, Tax Reform Options: Incentives for Capital Investment and Manufacturing, March 6, 2012, at http://www.finance.senate.gov/imo/media/doc/Testimony%20of%20Jane%20Gravelle.pdf.

In addition, there is some accelerated depreciation for buildings, primarily rental housing, but the revenue losses are largely for unincorporated businesses.

The Senate Finance Committee has released discussion drafts on cost recovery and accounting that relate to corporate taxation as well as a draft on international corporate tax issues.[52] These proposals have not been scored. The cost recovery provisions would introduce a new depreciation system that would slow depreciation and approximate the present value of economic depreciation. Assets would be added to general pools rather than each vintage of investments being depreciated separately. Real property would be depreciated over 43 years. Research and development expenses would be deducted in equal increments over five years, as would half of advertising expenditures (the remainder would continue to be deducted when incurred). Oil extraction expenses would be recovered over five years and percentage depletion would be repealed. LIFO and lower of cost of market inventory would be repealed (see discussion of LIFO below).

Production Activities Deduction

One of the larger tax expenditures outside of deferral is the production activities deduction, which allows a deduction of 9% of taxable income for domestic production for certain industries, primarily manufacturing, electricity and natural gas production, and construction. This provision would allow a corporate tax rate reduction of 0.7 percentage points. This provision has been criticized as distorting the tax treatment of different industries by granting differential tax rates. In addition, it creates administrative and compliance problems in both distinguishing domestic content and identifying eligible activities. About a quarter of the cost benefits unincorporated businesses and these revenues are included in the above estimate; without those revenues the reduction would be under a percentage point.[53]

The only reservation about this deduction is that it is more likely to apply to multinationals because of the industry restrictions and a revenue neutral substitution could raise the true statutory rate. For example, a 0.7 percentage point reduction in the federal rate would allow, after interacting with state taxes, a reduction from 39.2% to 38.5%, whereas firms with the production activities deduction have a rate of 36.3%. One option would be to tailor the provision more closely to the characteristics of multinationals, including disallowing the deduction for unincorporated businesses and further restricting the eligible activities (e.g., disallow electricity production as a qualified activity), and use those revenues to cut the rate, while retaining the deduction. If restricted to corporate manufacturing most than half of revenues would be recouped.[54]

---

[52] Senate Finance Committee, Baucus Works to Overhaul Outdated Tax Code, November 21 at http://www.finance.senate.gov/newsroom/chairman/release/?id=536eefeb-2ae2-453f-af9b-946c305d5c93.

[53] See CRS Report R41988, *The Section 199 Production Activities Deduction: Background and Analysis*, by Molly F. Sherlock. Statement Before the Senate Committee on Finance, Tax Reform Options: Incentives for Capital Investment and Manufacturing, March 6, 2012, at http://www.finance.senate.gov/imo/media/doc/Testimony%20of%20Jane%20Gravelle.pdf.

[54] Jane G. Gravelle Statement Before the Senate Committee on Finance, Tax Reform Options: Incentives for Capital Investment and Manufacturing, March 6, 2012, at http://www.finance.senate.gov/imo/media/doc/Testimony%20of%20Jane%20Gravelle.pdf.

Tax Treatment of Foreign Source Income

The largest tax expenditure is the deferral of tax on foreign source income, which would permit a corporate tax rate reduction of 3.1 percentage points. This move toward worldwide tax would also, independently, increase the amount of capital in the United States by discouraging outbound capital and would reduce the benefit of profit shifting mechanisms, perhaps significantly. A larger reduction would be possible, by about 4 percentage points or more if the foreign tax credit were limited to offsetting tax only on income earned in that country as was proposed in S. 3018, 111th Congress.[55] This change would eliminate most cross-crediting and raise more revenue; it would also be projected to gain a similar amount in welfare gain to the rate cut itself.[56]

Other revenue raising alternatives affecting taxation of foreign source income have been proposed. President Obama has proposed a set of revisions that is estimated to raise $157 billion over 10 years: the major proposals are disallowing interest and certain other deductions of the parent company to the extent income abroad is not taxed currently ($37 billion), limiting foreign tax credits that can offset income to the same share as the share of income repatriated ($66 billion), a provision to tax excess returns of intangibles ($26 billion), and limiting foreign tax credits for certain extractive companies ($10 billion). These provisions would allow a rate cut of about a percentage point.[57] An alternative would be to move to an actual territorial tax that exempts all active income earned abroad but disallows part of overhead expenses of parent companies, which is estimated to raise $76 billion[58] and allow a rate cut of 0.5 percentage points. There are many other revisions to the treatment of foreign source income that would raise varying amounts of revenue.[59]

House Ways and Means Chairman Camp has proposed a territorial tax (revenue neutral) that would preclude any revenue gains from the tax treatment of foreign source income.[60] The Senate Finance Committee has released d a discussion draft on international corporate tax issue. All foreign source income would be subject to tax (equivalent to repealing deferral) but some income would be taxed at a lower rate than the statutory rate (i.e., a minimum tax would be imposed).[61] This proposal has not been scored but could raise revenue, depending on the minimum tax rate.

---

[55] Estimate from Joint Committee on Taxation scoring of S. 3018, 111th Congress, at http://www.wyden.senate.gov/ download/joint-committee-on-taxation-estimated-score-of-the-bipartisan-tax-fairness-and-simplification-act-of-2010. This estimate could be larger, since it was prepared before JCT increased the revenue effect of deferral.

[56] For revenue estimates and analysis of this provisions, see Jane G. Gravelle, "International Tax Policy: Are We Heading in the Right Direction?," December 2010, Forthcoming in the Proceedings of the National Tax Association. This provision should raise about $60 billion of revenue a year, much more than eliminating deferral alone. Note that further measures might need to be taken to prevent corporations from inverting (moving their headquarters abroad), although current rules are already in place that appear to have been effective in preventing these inversions.

[57] U.S. Department of the Treasury, *General Explanations of the Administration's Fiscal Year 2012 Revenue Proposals*, April, 2013, http://www.treasury.gov/resource-center/tax-policy/Documents/General-Explanations-FY2014.pdf.

[58] Estimates by the Joint Committee on Taxation as reported in Congressional Budget Office, *Reducing the Deficit: Spending and Revenue Options*, March 10, 2011, http://www.cbo.gov/ftpdocs/120xx/doc12085/03-10-ReducingTheDeficit.pdf.

[59] See CRS Report R40623, *Tax Havens: International Tax Avoidance and Evasion*, by Jane G. Gravelle, for a discussion. Other options include eliminating deferral and limiting tax credits for tax haven or low tax countries, requiring a share of foreign income to be repatriated, and formula apportionment.

[60] See CRS Report R42624, *Moving to a Territorial Income Tax: Options and Challenges*, by Jane G. Gravelle.

[61] Senate Finance Committee, Baucus Unveils Proposals for International Tax Reform, November 19, 2013, at http://www.finance.senate.gov/newsroom/chairman/release/?id=f946a9f3-d296-42ad-bae4-bcf451b34b14.

Revenue offsets that increase the taxation of foreign source income can be significant and reinforce the capital flow and welfare effects of a rate cut in a global economy. Whether revenue increases from the treatment of foreign source income can be used as revenue offsets is unclear. Most proponents of rate reductions are also strong opponents of increasing the tax on foreign source income, and indeed favor lowering that tax burden, perhaps by moving to a territorial system without cost allocation, which would likely lose a small amount of revenue.[62] Such a change would reduce capital investment in the United States, although probably slightly, and offset the capital flow and welfare gains of a rate cut.

The estimate in **Table 10** does not include the effect of deferral of active financing income, which is a temporary provision but has been extended for many years. It would increase the cost of deferral by about 10%.

LIFO Inventory Accounting

Another option is the repeal of LIFO (last in, first out) accounting, which allows firms to treat goods sold as the latest acquired; eliminating this provision would raise $97.5 billion over 10 years[63] and allow a 0.8 percentage point reduction in the corporate rate. Most firms do not use LIFO because they must conform tax and book methods.[64] There is, however, a justification for LIFO, in that, on average, it eliminates the tax on inflationary gains.[65]

Other Tax Expenditures and Base Broadening Provisions[66]

There are several remaining tax expenditures but most are either small or would be questionable as offsets for a variety of reasons.[67] If every corporate tax expenditure were repealed, including those mentioned previously, the corporate rate could be cut by 7.9 percentage points, to 27.1%, assuming no behavioral responses.[68] (In the category addressing the treatment of foreign source income, only the deferral provision is a tax expenditure.) Larger cuts could occur if the repeal of benefits for unincorporated businesses were used to cut corporate rates. Without revenue from the repeal of deferral, the rate would fall by approximately 5.5 percentage points, or to 29.5%

---

[62] See "Obama Backs Corporate Tax Cut If Won't Raise Deficit," *Bloomberg*, January 25, 2011, http://www.newsmax.com/Newsfront/ALLTOP-BB-BNALL-BNSTAFF/2011/01/25/id/383906.

[63] Ibid.

[64] Ibid.

[65] This proposal would also repeal another method, the lower of cost or market, which is more difficult to justify.

[66] Table 15 does not include an item for the title passage rule (inventory source sales rule) that allows a reduction of tax on foreign source income for firms with excess foreign tax credits. Indications are that this estimate has been reduced significantly, based on data in the most recent CBO options study, See Congressional Budget Office,(2011) Reducing the Deficit: Spending and Revenue Options, http://www.cbo.gov/ftpdocs/120xx/doc12085/03-10-ReducingTheDeficit.pdf.

[67] Most of these are discussed in Jane G. Gravelle, "Practical Tax Reform for a More Efficient System, *Virginia Tax Review*," vol. 30, fall 2010, pp. 389-406.

[68] Based on sums for FY2012-FY2014, reported in U.S. Committee on the Budget, *Tax Expenditures: Compendium of Background Material on Individual Provisions*, December 2010, compared with revenue projections as adjusted, for the same years. See http://www.gpo.gov/fdsys/pkg/CPRT-111SPRT62799/pdf/CPRT-111SPRT62799.pdf. Using these years avoids the effects of bonus depreciation.

The Joint Committee on Taxation estimates a rate of 28% for repeal of corporate preferences excluding deferral, but this estimate allows for higher gains from depreciation and expensing of research and development during the budget horizon. (They note this rate would not be revenue neutral in the long run).

The incentives for research and development are popular provisions that have some economic justification, and, in the case of expensing, would be extremely difficult to administer. Only the expensing provision is reflected in **Table 10**, but the research credit, which is temporary (and which the President proposes to make permanent, is actually larger. Special provisions for insurance companies are almost the size of the title passage rule, and would be an option as would the relatively smaller provisions for fossil fuels. The President's budget proposals would restrict insurance company provisions for a $14 billion gain (0.1 percentage point) and benefits for fossil fuels for a $43.6 billion gain (0.3 percentage points).[69] Provisions such as tax-exempt bonds or the low-income housing credit are, however, designed to benefit others (state and local governments or low-income tenants) and if the corporate benefit were removed, these activities would largely migrate to the unincorporated sector. Lower rates for small corporations would allow a 0.3 percentage point reduction. Taxing income of credit unions would allow less than 0.1 percentage points. There are a number of energy subsidies that are directed at conservation whose repeal is not generally considered, as is the case for corporate charitable deductions.

In addition, there are also some tax reform possibilities that are not in the tax expenditure budget. For example, a tax reform bill introduced by then-Chairman of the Ways and Means Committee Rangel in the 110th Congress (H.R. 3970) included a provision extending the write period for acquired intangibles that raised $20 billion over 10 years.[70]

Limits on Interest Deductions

Restricting the deduction of interest would permit a significant reduction in rates. Although the benefits vary with expected inflation, disallowing the deduction for the inflation portion of interest is estimated to allow a reduction of the tax rate in the neighborhood of 2.5 percentage points and, in a closed economy, would be an efficient reform.[71] It might also reduce the use of debt as a method of profit shifting (by borrowing in high tax countries).

There is, however, a reservation about this change when considering international capital flows: a revenue neutral change could decrease the net inflow of capital if debt is more mobile than equity.

Shifts Between Individual and Corporate Taxes: Restrictions on Using the Non-Corporate Form, and Shifting Tax Burdens to the Shareholder Level

According to a Treasury study, the share of business income that is in corporate form has declined from 80% to 50% since the early 1980s, primarily through the increase in the number of shareholders for small corporations that are allowed to elect partnership treatment (Subchapter S

---

[69] *General Explanations of the Administration's Fiscal Year 2012 Revenue Proposals*, U.S. Department of Treasury, February 2011.

[70] See CRS Report RL34229, *Corporate Tax Reform: Issues for Congress*, by Jane G. Gravelle, for a list of provisions in H.R. 3970.

[71] See CRS Report RL34229, *Corporate Tax Reform: Issues for Congress*, by Jane G. Gravelle.

corporations) and the growth in new organizational forms such as limited liability corporations that are taxed as partnerships.[72] Using the tax rates currently in effect, if all business owners moving to this form are in the top 35% tax bracket, and if dividends and capital gains are distributed and realized based on economy wide averages as well as being subject to the current 15% rate, returning to the early 1980s share would allow a rate cut of 3 percentage points without altering overall individual and corporate revenue.[73] Note, however, that the contribution to rate reduction declines rapidly as the corporate rate is cut. For example, a base broadening provision, such as those discussed above, that allowed a 3 percentage point rate cut starting at a 35% rate would allow a 2.6 percentage point reduction applying to a 30% rate and a 2.3 percentage point reduction starting at a 25% rate. The effect of moving operations to corporate form depends on the differential between the individual and corporate tax, and would reduce the rate by 1.3 percentage points starting at a 30% corporate rate, and actually raise the corporate rate if starting at a 25% rate.

This potential rate reduction is larger, however, if the individual rate is lower. According to estimates, the average tax rate for all partnership and Subchapter S income is 30%.[74] In that case, the percentage point reductions are 5, 2.3, and 1.5, respectively, beginning at a 35%, 30%, and 25% corporate tax rate. Because these shifts into the noncorporate sector are driven by new forms of large companies, it is likely that the tax rate is higher than average for partnership and Subchapter S income (many partnerships, for example, are no different from proprietorships except they have two owners instead of one), but probably lower than the top rate.

In a global economy, it is better to allow tax cuts within the corporate sector at the corporate rather than the individual level. One option is rolling back the 2003 cuts in dividends and capital gains, which would allow a rate cut of about 2.5 percentage points, and perhaps as much as 4 percentage points.[75] These increases in rates are scheduled to occur after 2012 when the Bush tax cuts expire, however, and whether they can be counted as revenue raisers depends on scoring options.

The last two options interact, however. The more taxes are collected at the individual level by raising taxes on dividends and capital gains, the larger a rate reduction from shifting income into the corporate sectors. If dividends were taxed at full rates and capital gains at 20%, then at a 30%

---

[72] United States Department of the Treasury, "Treasury Tax Conference on Business Taxation and Global Competitiveness: Background Paper," July 30, 2007, at http://www.ustreas.gov/press/releases/hp500 htm.

[73] To be revenue neutral, the new corporate tax plus the tax on after tax earnings of shareholders, which is t(B+dB) +ts(1-t)dB, where t is the corporate tax, ts is the tax at the shareholder level, B is the base and dB is the change in the base, must be equal to the current corporate tax less the individual tax on the change in base. The calculations assume that four-seventh of the corporate steady state return is paid in dividends, that half of capital gains is realized and that none of the earnings are in tax exempt forms such as IRAs, 401(k)s or pension funds.

[74] Weighted marginal tax rate based on data by the Tax Policy Center, Table T10-0211, http://www.taxpolicycenter.org/numbers/displayatab.cfm?DocID=2787.

[75] Based on estimates provided in the FY2011 budget proposals, indicating a revenue gain of $344.4 billion, $233.3 billion for dividends and $111.1 billion for capital gains. See "General Explanations of the Administration's Fiscal 2011 Revenue Proposals," February 2010, at http://www.treasury.gov/resource-center/tax-olicy/Documents/ greenbk10.pdf. Because these changes do not affect the corporate base and interact with the corporate rate change, the estimate is the percentage of revenue times the tax rate. This estimate was for a year earlier, so was increased by 5% to reflect economic growth. These estimates assume a large realizations elasticity, and would be considerably higher if that elasticity were reduced to levels consistent with recent empirical research. Based on data in CRS Report R41364, *Capital Gains Tax Options: Behavioral Responses and Revenues*, by Jane G. Gravelle, Table 2, the capital gains revenue would increase from $13.9 billion in 2019 to $33.1 billion, if lower elasticties are used. That implies the $111.1 billion would be higher and would permit a reduction of 3.6 percentage points.

---

individual tax rate and a 35% corporate rate, the reduction is 6.5 percentage points. These effects depend as well, of course, on how the individual tax rate on ordinary income develops, which is currently scheduled to rise.

Summing Up

This section has identified enough provisions to allow the corporate tax rate to be reduced to 25% without losing revenue over the long run (i.e., that do not depend on large short-run gains, such as those from reducing accelerated depreciation), but that would require going beyond corporate tax expenditures (which would account for only 5 percentage points) to business preferences associated with unincorporated businesses, foreign tax credit restrictions, or more fundamental reforms.

Appendix. Statutory Tax Rates, 1981-2010

Table A-1. Statutory Tax Rates in the United States and the Rest of the OECD Countries, 1981-2020

Year	United States	OECD Unweighted	OECD Weighted	OECD Weighted Fixed Countries
1981	49.7	47.8	49.6	49.6
1982	49.7	48.4	50.1	50.2
1983	49.8	48.3	50.5	50.6
1984	49.8	48.2	50.2	50.2
1985	49.8	48.6	50.0	50.0
1986	49.8	47.7	49.0	49.1
1987	44.2	47.3	48.7	48.8
1988	38.6	45.0	47.4	47.5
1989	38.7	43.4	46.2	46.2
1990	38.7	44.3	43.2	44.3
1991	38.9	39.7	44.1	42.2
1992	38.9	38.0	43.8	43.9
1993	39.8	37.6	43.1	43.2
1994	39.7	37.1	42.4	42.6
1995	39.6	36.6	43.1	43.5
1996	39.5	36.6	43.1	43.5
1997	39.5	36.6	43.3	43.8
1998	39.4	35.5	40.8	41.1
1999	39.4	34.6	38.8	39.1
2000	39.3	33.4	37.6	38.6
2001	39.3	32.2	35.5	36.1
2002	39.3	31.0	35	35.8
2003	39.3	30.7	34.6	35.5
2004	39.3	29.4	33.8	34.7
2005	39.3	28.3	33.1	34.3
2006	39.3	27.7	32.5	34.1
2007	39.3	27.2	32.0	35.8
2008	39.3	25.8	29.8	31.2
2009	39.1	25.6	29.6	31.2
2010	39.2	25.5	29.6	31.2

Source: Statutory tax rates and GDP, Organisation for Economic Co-operation and Development (OECD), http://www.oecd.org/dataoecd/26/56/33717459.xls and http://stats.oecd.org/Index.aspx?DatasetCode= SNA_TABLE1.

Note: The table provides the data incorporated into **Figure 1**; the OECD weighted line in that figure uses fixed countries.

Author Contact Information

Jane G. Gravelle
Senior Specialist in Economic Policy
jgravelle@crs.loc.gov, 7-7829